On the Move

This Planner Belongs to

_____

_____

DEDICATION

This book is dedicated to all the ambitious and organized people out there who are getting ready to move and want the move to go as smoothly as possible.

Your are my inspiration for producing books and I'm honored to be a part of keeping all your moving notes and checklists all in one place.

This journal notebook will help you record your details, of each room and each box as you prepare for your move.

Thoughtfully put together with these sections to record: Move Date, Moving Companies, Moving Checklists, Moving Instructions, Packing Contents Pages & Things To Sell.

HOW TO USE THIS BOOK

The purpose of this book is to keep all of your lists and notes all in one place. It will help keep you organized.

This Moving Checklist Journal will allow you to accurately document room by room, box by box and all the things you don't want to forget. It's a great way to chart your course through a smooth move.

Here are examples of the prompts for you to fill in and write about yourself in this book:

1. Move Date - where you're moving from and where you're moving to
2. Moving Companies - Company Contact Name, Address, Phone Number, Email, Cost/Quote, Availability & Notes
3. Moving Checklists - Your list of things to do 2 months, 6 weeks, 1 month, 2 weeks, 3 days before moving day & on moving day.
4. Moving Instructions For Each Room With Floor Plan Grid - Each room (place for 15 rooms) has space for name of the room and measurements along with furniture checklist & check box/item checklist. Each instruction page is followed by a blank grid page to sketch the layout of furniture. Also has a notes section at the bottom of each floor plan page.
5. Packing Contents Pages -Several pages of lists of box number and inventory of what's in each box.
6. Things To Sell - List your item, price and buyer.

Moving

Moving On the

_____

Moving From

_____

_____

Moving To

_____

_____

Moving Companies

Company Name:

Address:

Phone Number:

Email:

Cost/Quote:

Availability:

Notes:

Company Name:

Address:

Phone Number:

Email:

Cost/Quote:

Availability:

Notes:

Moving Companies

Company Name:

Address:

Phone Number:

Email:

Cost/Quote:

Availability:

Notes:

Company Name:

Address:

Phone Number:

Email:

Cost/Quote:

Availability:

Notes:

Moving Companies

Company Name:

Address:

Phone Number:

Email:

Cost/Quote:

Availability:

Notes:

Company Name:

Address:

Phone Number:

Email:

Cost/Quote:

Availability:

Notes:

Moving Checklist

2 Months Before

▪	▪	▪
▪	▪	▪
▪	▪	▪
▪	▪	▪
▪	▪	▪
▪	▪	▪

6 Weeks Before

▪	▪	▪
▪	▪	▪
▪	▪	▪
▪	▪	▪
▪	▪	▪
▪	▪	▪

Moving Checklist

1 Month Before

▪	▪	▪
▪	▪	▪
▪	▪	▪
▪	▪	▪
▪	▪	▪
▪	▪	▪

2 Weeks Before

▪	▪	▪
▪	▪	▪
▪	▪	▪
▪	▪	▪
▪	▪	▪
▪	▪	▪

Moving Checklist

3 Days Before

▪	▪	▪
▪	▪	▪
▪	▪	▪
▪	▪	▪
▪	▪	▪
▪	▪	▪

On the Day of the Move

▪	▪	▪
▪	▪	▪
▪	▪	▪
▪	▪	▪
▪	▪	▪
▪	▪	▪

Moving Instructions

Room:

Room
Height

Room
Depth

Room
Width

Furniture Checklist

▪	▪	▪
▪	▪	▪
▪	▪	▪
▪	▪	▪
▪	▪	▪
▪	▪	▪

Box/Items Checklist

▪	▪	▪
▪	▪	▪
▪	▪	▪
▪	▪	▪
▪	▪	▪
▪	▪	▪

Floor Plan

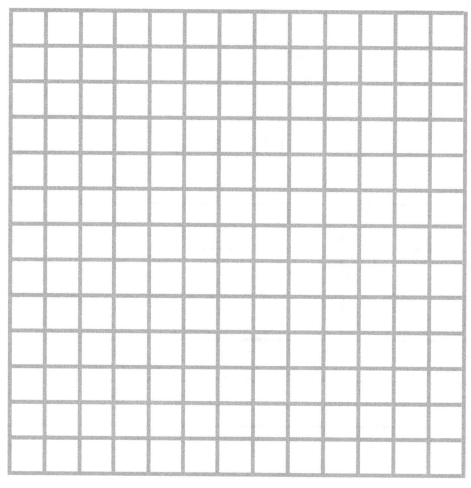

Notes/Moving Instructions

_____
_____
_____
_____
_____
_____
_____
_____

Moving Instructions

Room:

Room Height

Room Depth

Room Width

Furniture Checklist

■	■	■
■	■	■
■	■	■
■	■	■
■	■	■
■	■	■

Box/Items Checklist

■	■	■
■	■	■
■	■	■
■	■	■
■	■	■
■	■	■

Floor Plan

Notes/Moving Instructions

Moving Instructions

Room:

Room Height

Room Depth

Room Width

Furniture Checklist

▪	▪	▪
▪	▪	▪
▪	▪	▪
▪	▪	▪
▪	▪	▪
▪	▪	▪

Box/Items Checklist

▪	▪	▪
▪	▪	▪
▪	▪	▪
▪	▪	▪
▪	▪	▪
▪	▪	▪

Floor Plan

Notes/Moving Instructions

Moving Instructions

Room: _____

Room
Height _____   Room
Depth _____   Room
Width _____

Furniture Checklist

■	■	■
■	■	■
■	■	■
■	■	■
■	■	■
■	■	■

Box/Items Checklist

■	■	■
■	■	■
■	■	■
■	■	■
■	■	■
■	■	■

Floor Plan

Notes/Moving Instructions

Moving Instructions

Room:

Room Height

Room Depth

Room Width

Furniture Checklist

■	■	■
■	■	■
■	■	■
■	■	■
■	■	■
■	■	■

Box/Items Checklist

■	■	■
■	■	■
■	■	■
■	■	■
■	■	■
■	■	■

Floor Plan

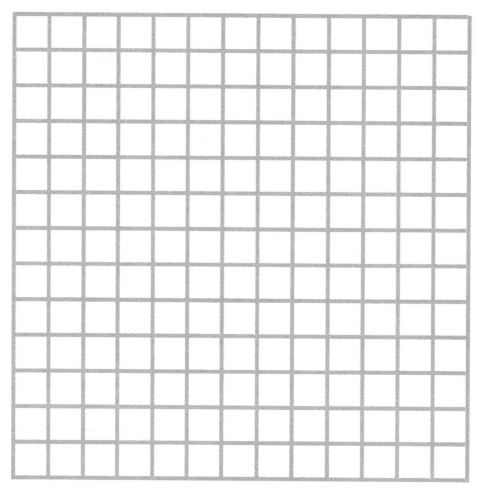

Notes/Moving Instructions

Moving Instructions

Room:

Room Height

Room Depth

Room Width

Furniture Checklist

▪	▪	▪
▪	▪	▪
▪	▪	▪
▪	▪	▪
▪	▪	▪
▪	▪	▪

Box/Items Checklist

▪	▪	▪
▪	▪	▪
▪	▪	▪
▪	▪	▪
▪	▪	▪
▪	▪	▪

Floor Plan

Notes/Moving Instructions

_____
_____
_____
_____
_____
_____
_____

Moving Instructions

Room:

Room Height

Room Depth

Room Width

Furniture Checklist		
■	■	■
■	■	■
■	■	■
■	■	■
■	■	■
■	■	■

Box/Items Checklist		
■	■	■
■	■	■
■	■	■
■	■	■
■	■	■
■	■	■

Floor Plan

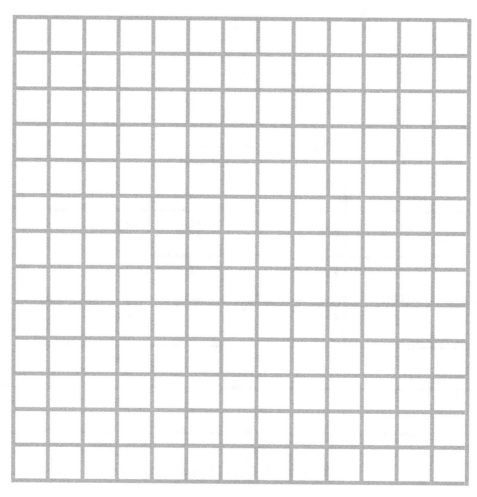

Notes/Moving Instructions

_____

_____

_____

_____

_____

_____

_____

_____

Moving Instructions

Room: _____

Room Height _____

Room Depth _____

Room Width _____

Furniture Checklist

■	■	■
■	■	■
■	■	■
■	■	■
■	■	■
■	■	■

Box/Items Checklist

■	■	■
■	■	■
■	■	■
■	■	■
■	■	■
■	■	■

Floor Plan

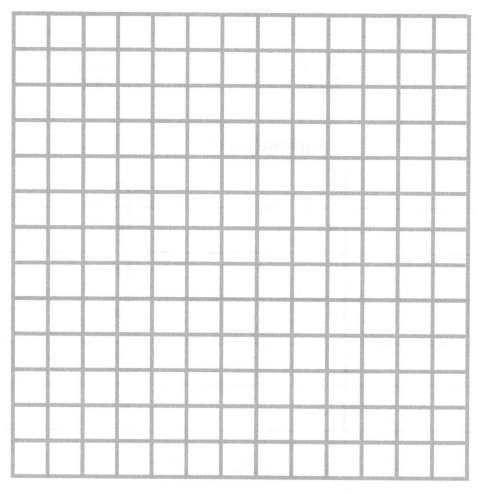

Notes/Moving Instructions

_____

_____

_____

_____

_____

_____

_____

Moving Instructions

Room:

Room Height

Room Depth

Room Width

Furniture Checklist

▪	▪	▪
▪	▪	▪
▪	▪	▪
▪	▪	▪
▪	▪	▪
▪	▪	▪

Box/Items Checklist

▪	▪	▪
▪	▪	▪
▪	▪	▪
▪	▪	▪
▪	▪	▪
▪	▪	▪

Floor Plan

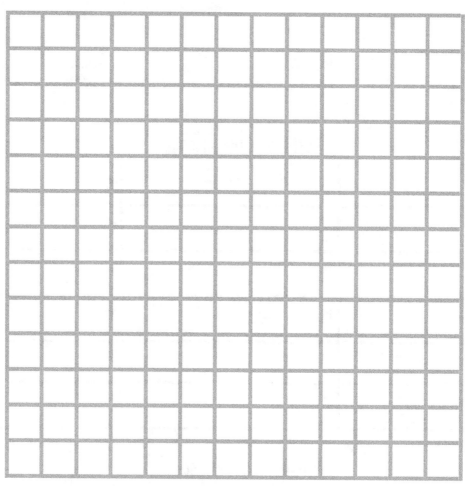

Notes/Moving Instructions

_____

_____

_____

_____

_____

_____

_____

_____

Moving Instructions

Room:

Room Height

Room Depth

Room Width

Furniture Checklist

■	■	■
■	■	■
■	■	■
■	■	■
■	■	■
■	■	■

Box/Items Checklist

■	■	■
■	■	■
■	■	■
■	■	■
■	■	■
■	■	■

Floor Plan

Notes/Moving Instructions

_____

_____

_____

_____

_____

_____

_____

Moving Instructions

Room:

Room Height

Room Depth

Room Width

Furniture Checklist		
▪	▪	▪
▪	▪	▪
▪	▪	▪
▪	▪	▪
▪	▪	▪
▪	▪	▪

Box/Items Checklist		
▪	▪	▪
▪	▪	▪
▪	▪	▪
▪	▪	▪
▪	▪	▪
▪	▪	▪

Floor Plan

Notes/Moving Instructions

Moving Instructions

Room:

Room Height:

Room Depth:

Room Width:

Furniture Checklist

☐	☐	☐
☐	☐	☐
☐	☐	☐
☐	☐	☐
☐	☐	☐
☐	☐	☐

Box/Items Checklist

☐	☐	☐
☐	☐	☐
☐	☐	☐
☐	☐	☐
☐	☐	☐
☐	☐	☐

Floor Plan

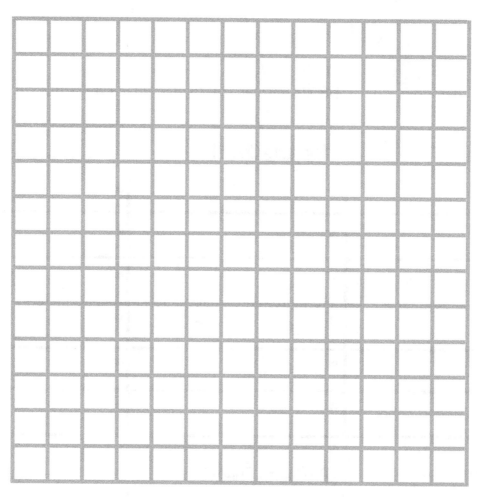

Notes/Moving Instructions

_____

_____

_____

_____

_____

_____

_____

Moving Instructions

Room:

Room Height

Room Depth

Room Width

Furniture Checklist		
■	■	■
■	■	■
■	■	■
■	■	■
■	■	■
■	■	■

Box/Items Checklist		
■	■	■
■	■	■
■	■	■
■	■	■
■	■	■
■	■	■

Floor Plan

Notes/Moving Instructions

_____

_____

_____

_____

_____

_____

_____

_____

Moving Instructions

Room:

Room Height

Room Depth

Room Width

Furniture Checklist

■	■	■
■	■	■
■	■	■
■	■	■
■	■	■
■	■	■

Box/Items Checklist

■	■	■
■	■	■
■	■	■
■	■	■
■	■	■
■	■	■

Floor Plan

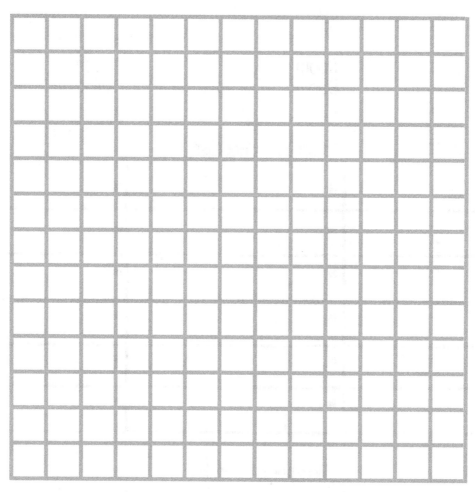

Notes/Moving Instructions

_____

_____

_____

_____

_____

_____

_____

_____

Moving Instructions

Room:

Room Height: Room Depth: Room Width:

Furniture Checklist

▪	▪	▪
▪	▪	▪
▪	▪	▪
▪	▪	▪
▪	▪	▪
▪	▪	▪

Box/Items Checklist

▪	▪	▪
▪	▪	▪
▪	▪	▪
▪	▪	▪
▪	▪	▪
▪	▪	▪

Packing Contents

Box Number:		
▪	▪	▪
▪	▪	▪
▪	▪	▪
▪	▪	▪
▪	▪	▪
▪	▪	▪

Box Number:		
▪	▪	▪
▪	▪	▪
▪	▪	▪
▪	▪	▪
▪	▪	▪
▪	▪	▪

Packing Contents

Box Number:		
■	■	■
■	■	■
■	■	■
■	■	■
■	■	■
■	■	■

Box Number:		
■	■	■
■	■	■
■	■	■
■	■	■
■	■	■
■	■	■

Packing Contents

Box Number:

∎	∎	∎
∎	∎	∎
∎	∎	∎
∎	∎	∎
∎	∎	∎
∎	∎	∎

Box Number:

∎	∎	∎
∎	∎	∎
∎	∎	∎
∎	∎	∎
∎	∎	∎
∎	∎	∎

Packing Contents

Box Number:

▪	▪	▪
▪	▪	▪
▪	▪	▪
▪	▪	▪
▪	▪	▪
▪	▪	▪

Box Number:

▪	▪	▪
▪	▪	▪
▪	▪	▪
▪	▪	▪
▪	▪	▪
▪	▪	▪

Packing Contents

Box Number:

■	■	■
■	■	■
■	■	■
■	■	■
■	■	■
■	■	■

Box Number:

■	■	■
■	■	■
■	■	■
■	■	■
■	■	■
■	■	■

Packing Contents

Box Number:		
■	■	■
■	■	■
■	■	■
■	■	■
■	■	■
■	■	■

Box Number:		
■	■	■
■	■	■
■	■	■
■	■	■
■	■	■
■	■	■

Packing Contents

Box Number:

■	■	■
■	■	■
■	■	■
■	■	■
■	■	■
■	■	■

Box Number:

■	■	■
■	■	■
■	■	■
■	■	■
■	■	■
■	■	■

Packing Contents

Box Number:

▪	▪	▪
▪	▪	▪
▪	▪	▪
▪	▪	▪
▪	▪	▪
▪	▪	▪

Box Number:

▪	▪	▪
▪	▪	▪
▪	▪	▪
▪	▪	▪
▪	▪	▪
▪	▪	▪

Packing Contents

Box Number:		
▪	▪	▪
▪	▪	▪
▪	▪	▪
▪	▪	▪
▪	▪	▪
▪	▪	▪

Box Number:		
▪	▪	▪
▪	▪	▪
▪	▪	▪
▪	▪	▪
▪	▪	▪
▪	▪	▪

Packing Contents

Box Number:

■	■	■
■	■	■
■	■	■
■	■	■
■	■	■
■	■	■

Box Number:

■	■	■
■	■	■
■	■	■
■	■	■
■	■	■
■	■	■

Packing Contents

Box Number:		
▪	▪	▪
▪	▪	▪
▪	▪	▪
▪	▪	▪
▪	▪	▪
▪	▪	▪

Box Number:		
▪	▪	▪
▪	▪	▪
▪	▪	▪
▪	▪	▪
▪	▪	▪
▪	▪	▪

Packing Contents

Box Number:		
■	■	■
■	■	■
■	■	■
■	■	■
■	■	■
■	■	■

Box Number:		
■	■	■
■	■	■
■	■	■
■	■	■
■	■	■
■	■	■

Packing Contents

Box Number:		
■	■	■
■	■	■
■	■	■
■	■	■
■	■	■
■	■	■

Box Number:		
■	■	■
■	■	■
■	■	■
■	■	■
■	■	■
■	■	■

Packing Contents

Box Number:		
▪	▪	▪
▪	▪	▪
▪	▪	▪
▪	▪	▪
▪	▪	▪
▪	▪	▪

Box Number:		
▪	▪	▪
▪	▪	▪
▪	▪	▪
▪	▪	▪
▪	▪	▪
▪	▪	▪

Packing Contents

Box Number:

■	■	■
■	■	■
■	■	■
■	■	■
■	■	■
■	■	■

Box Number:

■	■	■
■	■	■
■	■	■
■	■	■
■	■	■
■	■	■

Packing Contents

Box Number:

∎	∎	∎
∎	∎	∎
∎	∎	∎
∎	∎	∎
∎	∎	∎
∎	∎	∎

Box Number:

∎	∎	∎
∎	∎	∎
∎	∎	∎
∎	∎	∎
∎	∎	∎
∎	∎	∎

Packing Contents

Box Number:

▪	▪	▪
▪	▪	▪
▪	▪	▪
▪	▪	▪
▪	▪	▪
▪	▪	▪

Box Number:

▪	▪	▪
▪	▪	▪
▪	▪	▪
▪	▪	▪
▪	▪	▪
▪	▪	▪

Packing Contents

Box Number:

■	■	■
■	■	■
■	■	■
■	■	■
■	■	■
■	■	■

Box Number:

■	■	■
■	■	■
■	■	■
■	■	■
■	■	■
■	■	■

Packing Contents

Box Number:		
▪	▪	▪
▪	▪	▪
▪	▪	▪
▪	▪	▪
▪	▪	▪
▪	▪	▪

Box Number:		
▪	▪	▪
▪	▪	▪
▪	▪	▪
▪	▪	▪
▪	▪	▪
▪	▪	▪

Packing Contents

Box Number:		
▪	▪	▪
▪	▪	▪
▪	▪	▪
▪	▪	▪
▪	▪	▪
▪	▪	▪

Box Number:		
▪	▪	▪
▪	▪	▪
▪	▪	▪
▪	▪	▪
▪	▪	▪
▪	▪	▪

Packing Contents

Box Number:		
▪	▪	▪
▪	▪	▪
▪	▪	▪
▪	▪	▪
▪	▪	▪
▪	▪	▪

Box Number:		
▪	▪	▪
▪	▪	▪
▪	▪	▪
▪	▪	▪
▪	▪	▪
▪	▪	▪

Packing Contents

Box Number:		
■	■	■
■	■	■
■	■	■
■	■	■
■	■	■
■	■	■

Box Number:		
■	■	■
■	■	■
■	■	■
■	■	■
■	■	■
■	■	■

Packing Contents

Box Number:		
▪	▪	▪
▪	▪	▪
▪	▪	▪
▪	▪	▪
▪	▪	▪
▪	▪	▪

Box Number:		
▪	▪	▪
▪	▪	▪
▪	▪	▪
▪	▪	▪
▪	▪	▪
▪	▪	▪

Packing Contents

Box Number:

▪	▪	▪
▪	▪	▪
▪	▪	▪
▪	▪	▪
▪	▪	▪
▪	▪	▪

Box Number:

▪	▪	▪
▪	▪	▪
▪	▪	▪
▪	▪	▪
▪	▪	▪
▪	▪	▪

Packing Contents

Box Number:

▪	▪	▪
▪	▪	▪
▪	▪	▪
▪	▪	▪
▪	▪	▪
▪	▪	▪

Box Number:

▪	▪	▪
▪	▪	▪
▪	▪	▪
▪	▪	▪
▪	▪	▪
▪	▪	▪

Packing Contents

Box Number:		
■	■	■
■	■	■
■	■	■
■	■	■
■	■	■
■	■	■

Box Number:		
■	■	■
■	■	■
■	■	■
■	■	■
■	■	■
■	■	■

Packing Contents

Box Number:

▪	▪	▪
▪	▪	▪
▪	▪	▪
▪	▪	▪
▪	▪	▪
▪	▪	▪

Box Number:

▪	▪	▪
▪	▪	▪
▪	▪	▪
▪	▪	▪
▪	▪	▪
▪	▪	▪

Packing Contents

Box Number:		
∎	∎	∎
∎	∎	∎
∎	∎	∎
∎	∎	∎
∎	∎	∎
∎	∎	∎

Box Number:		
∎	∎	∎
∎	∎	∎
∎	∎	∎
∎	∎	∎
∎	∎	∎
∎	∎	∎

Packing Contents

Box Number:		
■	■	■
■	■	■
■	■	■
■	■	■
■	■	■
■	■	■

Box Number:		
■	■	■
■	■	■
■	■	■
■	■	■
■	■	■
■	■	■

Packing Contents

Box Number:		
▪	▪	▪
▪	▪	▪
▪	▪	▪
▪	▪	▪
▪	▪	▪
▪	▪	▪

Box Number:		
▪	▪	▪
▪	▪	▪
▪	▪	▪
▪	▪	▪
▪	▪	▪
▪	▪	▪

Packing Contents

Box Number:

▪	▪	▪
▪	▪	▪
▪	▪	▪
▪	▪	▪
▪	▪	▪
▪	▪	▪

Box Number:

▪	▪	▪
▪	▪	▪
▪	▪	▪
▪	▪	▪
▪	▪	▪
▪	▪	▪

Packing Contents

Box Number:		
■	■	■
■	■	■
■	■	■
■	■	■
■	■	■
■	■	■

Box Number:		
■	■	■
■	■	■
■	■	■
■	■	■
■	■	■
■	■	■

Packing Contents

Box Number:

■	■	■
■	■	■
■	■	■
■	■	■
■	■	■
■	■	■

Box Number:

■	■	■
■	■	■
■	■	■
■	■	■
■	■	■
■	■	■

Packing Contents

Box Number:

▪	▪	▪
▪	▪	▪
▪	▪	▪
▪	▪	▪
▪	▪	▪
▪	▪	▪

Box Number:

▪	▪	▪
▪	▪	▪
▪	▪	▪
▪	▪	▪
▪	▪	▪
▪	▪	▪

Packing Contents

Box Number:

■	■	■
■	■	■
■	■	■
■	■	■
■	■	■
■	■	■

Box Number:

■	■	■
■	■	■
■	■	■
■	■	■
■	■	■
■	■	■

Packing Contents

Box Number:

▪	▪	▪
▪	▪	▪
▪	▪	▪
▪	▪	▪
▪	▪	▪
▪	▪	▪

Box Number:

▪	▪	▪
▪	▪	▪
▪	▪	▪
▪	▪	▪
▪	▪	▪
▪	▪	▪

Packing Contents

Box Number:

■	■	■
■	■	■
■	■	■
■	■	■
■	■	■
■	■	■

Box Number:

■	■	■
■	■	■
■	■	■
■	■	■
■	■	■
■	■	■

Packing Contents

Box Number:		
■	■	■
■	■	■
■	■	■
■	■	■
■	■	■
■	■	■

Box Number:		
■	■	■
■	■	■
■	■	■
■	■	■
■	■	■
■	■	■

Packing Contents

Box Number:		
■	■	■
■	■	■
■	■	■
■	■	■
■	■	■
■	■	■

Box Number:		
■	■	■
■	■	■
■	■	■
■	■	■
■	■	■
■	■	■

Packing Contents

Box Number:		
▪	▪	▪
▪	▪	▪
▪	▪	▪
▪	▪	▪
▪	▪	▪
▪	▪	▪

Box Number:		
▪	▪	▪
▪	▪	▪
▪	▪	▪
▪	▪	▪
▪	▪	▪
▪	▪	▪

Packing Contents

Box Number:

■	■	■
■	■	■
■	■	■
■	■	■
■	■	■
■	■	■

Box Number:

■	■	■
■	■	■
■	■	■
■	■	■
■	■	■
■	■	■

Packing Contents

Box Number:		
■	■	■
■	■	■
■	■	■
■	■	■
■	■	■
■	■	■

Box Number:		
■	■	■
■	■	■
■	■	■
■	■	■
■	■	■
■	■	■

Things to Sell

ITEM TO SELL	PRICE	BUYER

Things to Sell

ITEM TO SELL	PRICE	BUYER

Things to Sell

ITEM TO SELL	PRICE	BUYER

Things to Sell

ITEM TO SELL	PRICE	BUYER

Things to Sell

ITEM TO SELL	PRICE	BUYER

Things to Sell

ITEM TO SELL	PRICE	BUYER

Things to Sell

ITEM TO SELL	PRICE	BUYER

Things to Sell

ITEM TO SELL	PRICE	BUYER

CPSIA information can be obtained
at www.ICGtesting.com
Printed in the USA
BVHW012001060820
585711BV00007B/153